The **Gospel** According to
Mark

VERITAS

The **Gospel** According to
Mark

(1:1–16:20)

Published 2011 by
Veritas Publications
7–8 Lower Abbey Street
Dublin 1, Ireland
publications@veritas.ie
www.veritas.ie

ISBN 978 1 84730 328 8
Copyright © Veritas, 2011

A catalogue record for this book is available from the British Library.

Text taken from the *New Revised Standard Version Bible* © 1989,
1995 by the Division of Christian Education of National Council of
the Churches of Christ in the United States of America. Used with
permission. All rights reserved.

Front cover image from the Bridgeman Art Library, 'Saint Mark' (oil on
copper) by Guercino (Giovanni Francesco Barbieri).
Designed by Norma Prause-Brewer, Veritas.
Printed in the Republic of Ireland by W & G Baird Ltd, Antrim.

Veritas books are printed on paper made from the wood pulp of
managed forests. For every tree felled, at least one tree is planted,
thereby renewing natural resources.

Contents

Preface 7

Introduction, Jesus' Baptism (1:1-13) 9

Ministry in Galilee (1:14–6:6a) 10

Apostolic Journeys (6:6b–9:50) 25

Journey to Jerusalem (10:1-52) 36

Ministry and Passion in Jerusalem (11:1–16:20) 40

Lectio divina 62

Index 64

The **Gospel** According to

Mark

(1:1–16:20)

Saint Mark • Guercino (Giovanni Francesco Barbieri)

PREFACE

The Gospel of Mark is the second book of the New Testament. It is noted for its simple and popular style, as well as a vividness of detail, which is consistent with it being an eyewitness account. The Gospel of Mark deals chiefly with the Galilean ministry of Jesus, and the events of the last week in Jerusalem. There is no recording of the birth of Jesus, or of some popular parables, such as the Sermon on the Mount, but action dominates throughout and a dramatic sense of urgency is present. Mark's Gospel was most likely meant to be read aloud to an assembly rather than privately. It is a Gospel of the ear rather than of the eye, with its frequent repetitions and summaries. The shortest Gospel, it is presumed to be the earliest written account of the life of Jesus, and so a primary source for the other Gospel writers.

'You are my Son, the Beloved; with you I am well pleased.'

INTRODUCTION, JESUS' BAPTISM (1:1-13)

chapter ONE

The **Proclamation** of John the Baptist

¹The beginning of the good news of Jesus Christ, the Son of God.
²As it is written in the prophet Isaiah,
'See, I am sending my messenger ahead of you, who will prepare your way;
³the voice of one crying out in the wilderness:
"Prepare the way of the Lord, make his paths straight,"'
⁴John the baptiser appeared in the wilderness, proclaiming a baptism of repentance for the forgiveness of sins. ⁵And people from the whole Judean countryside and all the people of Jerusalem were going out to him, and were baptised by him in the river Jordan, confessing their sins. ⁶Now John was clothed with camel's hair, with a leather belt around his waist, and he ate locusts and wild honey. ⁷He proclaimed, 'The one who is more powerful than I is coming after me; I am not worthy to stoop down and untie the thong of his sandals. ⁸I have baptised you with water; but he will baptise you with the Holy Spirit.'

The **Baptism** of Jesus

⁹In those days Jesus came from Nazareth of Galilee and was baptised by John in the Jordan. ¹⁰And just as he was coming up out of the water, he saw the heavens torn apart and the Spirit descending like a dove on him. ¹¹And a voice came from heaven, 'You are my Son, the Beloved; with you I am well pleased.'

The **Temptation** of Jesus

¹²And the Spirit immediately drove him out into the wilderness. ¹³He was in the wilderness forty days, tempted by Satan; and he was with the wild beasts; and the angels waited on him.

'Follow me and I will make you fish for people.'

MINISTRY IN GALILEE (1:14–6:6A)

The **Beginning** of the Galilean **Ministry**

¹⁴Now after John was arrested, Jesus came to Galilee, proclaiming the good news of God, ¹⁵and saying, 'The time is fulfilled, and the kingdom of God has come near; repent, and believe in the good news.'

Jesus calls the First **Disciples**

¹⁶As Jesus passed along the Sea of Galilee, he saw Simon and his brother Andrew casting a net into the sea – for they were fishermen. ¹⁷And Jesus said to them, 'Follow me and I will make you fish for people.' ¹⁸And immediately they left their nets and followed him. ¹⁹As he went a little farther, he saw James son of Zebedee and his brother John, who were in their boat mending the nets. ²⁰Immediately he called them; and they left their father Zebedee in the boat with the hired men, and followed him.

The Man with an Unclean **Spirit**

²¹They went to Capernaum; and when the sabbath came, he entered the synagogue and taught. ²²They were astounded at his teaching, for he taught them as one having authority, and not as the scribes. ²³Just then there was in their synagogue a man with an unclean spirit, ²⁴and he cried out, 'What have you to do with us, Jesus of Nazareth? Have you come to destroy us? I know who you are, the Holy One of God.' ²⁵But Jesus rebuked him, saying, 'Be silent, and come out of him!' ²⁶And the unclean spirit, convulsing him and crying with a loud voice, came out of him. ²⁷They were all amazed, and they kept on asking one another, 'What is this? A new teaching – with authority! He commands even the unclean spirits, and they obey him.' ²⁸At once his fame began to spread throughout the surrounding region of Galilee.

Jesus Heals Many at Simon's House

²⁹As soon as they left the synagogue, they entered the house of Simon and Andrew, with James and John. ³⁰Now Simon's mother-in-law was in bed with a fever, and they told him about her at once. ³¹He came and took her by the hand and lifted her up. Then the fever left her, and she began to serve them.
³²That evening, at sundown, they brought to him all who were sick or possessed with demons. ³³And the whole city was gathered around the door. ³⁴And he cured many who were sick with various diseases, and cast out many demons; and he would not permit the demons to speak, because they knew him.

A **Preaching** Tour in Galilee

35In the morning, while it was still very dark, he got up and went out to a deserted place, and there he prayed. 36And Simon and his companions hunted for him. 37When they found him, they said to him, 'Everyone is searching for you.' 38He answered, 'Let us go on to the neighbouring towns, so that I may proclaim the message there also; for that is what I came out to do.' 39And he went throughout Galilee, proclaiming the message in their synagogues and casting out demons.

Jesus Cleanses a Leper

40A leper came to him begging him, and kneeling he said to him, 'If you choose, you can make me clean.' 41Moved with pity, Jesus stretched out his hand and touched him, and said to him, 'I do choose. Be made clean!' 42Immediately the leprosy left him, and he was made clean. 43After sternly warning him he sent him away at once, 44saying to him, 'See that you say nothing to anyone; but go, show yourself to the priest, and offer for your cleansing what Moses commanded, as a testimony to them.' 45But he went out and began to proclaim it freely, and to spread the word, so that Jesus could no longer go into a town openly, but stayed out in the country; and people came to him from every quarter.

chapter TWO

Jesus Heals a Paralytic

1When he returned to Capernaum after some days, it was reported that he was at home. 2So many gathered around that there was no longer room for them, not even in front of the door; and he was speaking the word to them. 3Then some people came, bringing to him a paralysed man, carried by four of them. 4And when they could not bring him to Jesus because of the crowd, they removed the roof above him; and after having dug through it, they let down the mat on which the paralytic lay. 5When Jesus saw their faith, he said to the paralytic, 'Son, your sins are forgiven.' 6Now some of the scribes were sitting there, questioning in their hearts, 7'Why does this fellow speak in this way? It is blasphemy! Who can forgive sins but God alone?' 8At once Jesus perceived in his spirit that they were discussing these questions among themselves; and he said to them, 'Why do you raise such questions in your hearts? 9Which is easier, to say to the paralytic, "Your sins are forgiven," or to say, "Stand up and take your mat and walk"? 10But so that you may know that the Son of Man has authority on earth to forgive sins' – he said to the paralytic – 11'I say to you, stand up, take your mat and go to your home.' 12And he stood up, and immediately took the mat and went out before all of them; so that they were all amazed and glorified God, saying, 'We have never seen anything like this!'

'Why does he eat
with tax collectors
and sinners?'

Jesus Calls Levi

¹³Jesus went out again beside the sea; the whole crowd gathered around him, and he taught them. ¹⁴As he was walking along, he saw Levi son of Alphaeus sitting at the tax booth, and he said to him, 'Follow me.' And he got up and followed him. ¹⁵And as he sat at dinner in Levi's house, many tax collectors and sinners were also sitting with Jesus and his disciples – for there were many who followed him. ¹⁶When the scribes of the Pharisees saw that he was eating with sinners and tax collectors, they said to his disciples, 'Why does he eat with tax collectors and sinners?' ¹⁷When Jesus heard this, he said to them, 'Those who are well have no need of a physician, but those who are sick; I have come to call not the righteous but sinners.'

Pronouncement about the **Sabbath**

²³One sabbath he was going through the grainfields; and as they made their way his disciples began to pluck heads of grain. ²⁴The Pharisees said to him, 'Look, why are they doing what is not lawful on the sabbath?' ²⁵And he said to them, 'Have you never read what David did when he and his companions were hungry and in need of food? ²⁶He entered the house of God, when Abiathar was high priest, and ate the bread of the Presence, which it is not lawful for any but the priests to eat, and he gave some to his companions.' ²⁷Then he said to them, 'The sabbath was made for humankind, and not humankind for the sabbath; ²⁸so the Son of Man is lord even of the sabbath.'

The Question about **Fasting**

¹⁸Now John's disciples and the Pharisees were fasting; and people came and said to him, 'Why do John's disciples and the disciples of the Pharisees fast, but your disciples do not fast?' ¹⁹Jesus said to them, 'The wedding guests cannot fast while the bridegroom is with them, can they? As long as they have the bridegroom with them, they cannot fast. ²⁰The days will come when the bridegroom is taken away from them, and then they will fast on that day.
²¹'No one sews a piece of unshrunk cloth on an old cloak; otherwise, the patch pulls away from it, the new from the old, and a worse tear is made. ²²And no one puts new wine into old wineskins; otherwise, the wine will burst the skins, and the wine is lost, and so are the skins; but one puts new wine into fresh wineskins.'

chapter THREE

The Man with a Withered Hand

¹Again he entered the synagogue, and a man was there who had a withered hand. ²They watched him to see whether he would cure him on the sabbath, so that they might accuse him. ³And he said to the man who had the withered hand, 'Come forward.' ⁴Then he said to them, 'Is it lawful to do good or to do harm on the sabbath, to save life or to kill?' But they were silent. ⁵He looked around at them with anger; he was grieved at their hardness of heart and said to the man, 'Stretch out your hand.' He stretched it out, and his hand was restored. ⁶The Pharisees went out and immediately conspired with the Herodians against him, how to destroy him.

A Multitude at the Seaside

⁷Jesus departed with his disciples to the sea, and a great multitude from Galilee followed him; ⁸hearing all that he was doing, they came to him in great numbers from Judea, Jerusalem, Idumea, beyond the Jordan, and the region around Tyre and Sidon. ⁹He told his disciples to have a boat ready for him because of the crowd, so that they would not crush him; ¹⁰for he had cured many, so that all who had diseases pressed upon him to touch him. ¹¹Whenever the unclean spirits saw him, they fell down before him and shouted, 'You are the Son of God!' ¹²But he sternly ordered them not to make him known.

12

Apostles

Jesus Appoints **the Twelve**

¹³He went up the mountain and called to him those whom he wanted, and they came to him. ¹⁴And he appointed twelve, whom he also named apostles, to be with him, and to be sent out to proclaim the message, ¹⁵and to have authority to cast out demons. ¹⁶So he appointed the twelve: Simon (to whom he gave the name Peter); ¹⁷James son of Zebedee and John the brother of James (to whom he gave the name Boanerges, that is, Sons of Thunder); ¹⁸and Andrew, and Philip, and Bartholomew, and Matthew, and Thomas, and James son of Alphaeus, and Thaddaeus, and Simon the Cananaean, ¹⁹and Judas Iscariot, who betrayed him.

Jesus and Beelzebul

Then he went home; ²⁰and the crowd came together again, so that they could not even eat. ²¹When his family heard it, they went out to restrain him, for people were saying, 'He has gone out of his mind.' ²²And the scribes who came down from Jerusalem said, 'He has Beelzebul, and by the ruler of the demons he casts out demons.' ²³And he called them to him, and spoke to them in parables, 'How can Satan cast out Satan? ²⁴If a kingdom is divided against itself, that kingdom cannot stand. ²⁵And if a house is divided against itself, that house will not be able to stand. ²⁶And if Satan has risen up against himself and is divided, he cannot stand, but his end has come. ²⁷But no one can enter a strong man's house and plunder his property without first tying up the strong man; then indeed the house can be plundered. ²⁸'Truly I tell you, people will be forgiven for their sins and whatever blasphemies they utter; ²⁹but whoever blasphemes against the Holy Spirit can never have forgiveness, but is guilty of an eternal sin' – ³⁰for they had said, 'He has an unclean spirit.'

The **True Kindred** of Jesus

³¹Then his mother and his brothers came; and standing outside, they sent to him and called him. ³²A crowd was sitting around him; and they said to him, 'Your mother and your brothers and sisters are outside, asking for you.' ³³And he replied, 'Who are my mother and my brothers?' ³⁴And looking at those who sat around him, he said, 'Here are my mother and my brothers! ³⁵Whoever does the will of God is my brother and sister and mother.'

chapter FOUR

The Parable of the **Sower**

¹Again he began to teach beside the sea. Such a very large crowd gathered around him that he got into a boat on the sea and sat there, while the whole crowd was beside the sea on the land. ²He began to teach them many things in parables, and in his teaching he said to them: ³'Listen! A sower went out to sow. ⁴And as he sowed, some seed fell on the path, and the birds came and ate it up. ⁵Other seed fell on rocky ground, where it did not have much soil, and it sprang up quickly, since it had no depth of soil. ⁶And when the sun rose, it was scorched; and since it had no root, it withered away. ⁷Other seed fell among thorns, and the thorns grew up and choked it, and it yielded no grain. ⁸Other seed fell into good soil and brought forth grain, growing up and increasing and yielding thirty and sixty and a hundredfold.' ⁹And he said, 'Let anyone with ears to hear listen!'

The **Purpose of** the **Parables**

¹⁰When he was alone, those who were around him along with the twelve asked him about the parables. ¹¹And he said to them, 'To you has been given the secret of the kingdom of God, but for those outside, everything comes in parables; ¹²in order that
"they may indeed look, but not perceive,
and may indeed listen, but not understand;
so that they may not turn again and be forgiven."'
¹³And he said to them, 'Do you not understand this parable? Then how will you understand all the parables? ¹⁴The sower sows the word. ¹⁵These are the ones on the path where the word is sown: when they hear, Satan immediately comes and takes away the word that is sown in them. ¹⁶And these are the ones sown on rocky ground: when they hear the word, they immediately receive it with joy. ¹⁷But they have no root, and endure only for a while; then, when trouble or persecution arises on account of the word, immediately they fall away. ¹⁸And others are those sown among the thorns: these are the ones who hear the word, ¹⁹but the cares of the world, and the lure of wealth, and the desire for other things come in and choke the word, and it yields nothing. ²⁰And these are the ones sown on the good soil: they hear the word and accept it and bear fruit, thirty and sixty and a hundredfold.'

A **Lamp** under a Bushel Basket

²¹He said to them, 'Is a lamp brought in to be put under the bushel basket, or under the bed, and not on the lampstand? ²²For there is nothing hidden, except to be disclosed; nor is anything secret, except to come to light. ²³Let anyone with ears to hear listen!' ²⁴And he said to them, 'Pay attention to what you hear; the measure you give will be the measure you get, and still more will be given you. ²⁵For to those who have, more will be given; and from those who have nothing, even what they have will be taken away.'

The Parable of the Growing Seed

[26]He also said, 'The kingdom of God is as if someone would scatter seed on the ground, [27]and would sleep and rise night and day, and the seed would sprout and grow, he does not know how. [28]The earth produces of itself, first the stalk, then the head, then the full grain in the head. [29]But when the grain is ripe, at once he goes in with his sickle, because the harvest has come.'

The Parable of the Mustard Seed

[30]He also said, 'With what can we compare the kingdom of God, or what parable will we use for it? [31]It is like a mustard seed, which, when sown upon the ground, is the smallest of all the seeds on earth; [32]yet when it is sown it grows up and becomes the greatest of all shrubs, and puts forth large branches, so that the birds of the air can make nests in its shade.'

The Use of Parables

[33]With many such parables he spoke the word to them, as they were able to hear it; [34]he did not speak to them except in parables, but he explained everything in private to his disciples.

Jesus Stills a Storm

³⁵On that day, when evening had come, he said to them, 'Let us go across to the other side.' ³⁶And leaving the crowd behind, they took him with them in the boat, just as he was. Other boats were with him. ³⁷A great windstorm arose, and the waves beat into the boat, so that the boat was already being swamped. ³⁸But he was in the stern, asleep on the cushion; and they woke him up and said to him, 'Teacher, do you not care that we are perishing?' ³⁹He woke up and rebuked the wind, and said to the sea, 'Peace! Be still!' Then the wind ceased, and there was a dead calm. ⁴⁰He said to them, 'Why are you afraid? Have you still no faith?' ⁴¹And they were filled with great awe and said to one another, 'Who then is this, that even the wind and the sea obey him?'

'Why are you afraid?
Have you still no faith?'

CHAPTER **FIVE**

Jesus Heals the Gerasene Demoniac

¹They came to the other side of the sea, to the country of the Gerasenes. ²And when he had stepped out of the boat, immediately a man out of the tombs with an unclean spirit met him. ³He lived among the tombs; and no one could restrain him any more, even with a chain; ⁴for he had often been restrained with shackles and chains, but the chains he wrenched apart, and the shackles he broke in pieces; and no one had the strength to subdue him. ⁵Night and day among the tombs and on the mountains he was always howling and bruising himself with stones. ⁶When he saw Jesus from a distance, he ran and bowed down before him; ⁷and he shouted at the top of his voice, 'What have you to do with me, Jesus, Son of the Most High God? I adjure you by God, do not torment me.' ⁸For he had said to him,

'Come out of the man, you unclean spirit!' ⁹Then Jesus asked him, 'What is your name?' He replied, 'My name is Legion; for we are many.' ¹⁰He begged him earnestly not to send them out of the country. ¹¹Now there on the hillside a great herd of swine was feeding; ¹²and the unclean spirits begged him, 'Send us into the swine; let us enter them.' ¹³So he gave them permission. And the unclean spirits came out and entered the swine; and the herd, numbering about two thousand, rushed down the steep bank into the sea, and were drowned in the sea.

¹⁴The swineherds ran off and told it in the city and in the country. Then people came to see what it was that had happened. ¹⁵They came to Jesus and saw the demoniac sitting there, clothed and in his right mind, the very man who had had the legion; and they were afraid. ¹⁶Those who had seen what had happened to the demoniac and to the swine reported it. ¹⁷Then they began to beg Jesus to leave their neighbourhood. ¹⁸As he was getting into the boat, the man who had been possessed by demons begged him that he might be with him. ¹⁹But Jesus refused, and said to him, 'Go home to your friends, and tell them how much the Lord has done for you, and what mercy he has shown you.' ²⁰And he went away and began to proclaim in the Decapolis how much Jesus had done for him; and everyone was amazed.

A Girl Restored to Life and a **Woman Healed**

²¹When Jesus had crossed again in the boat to the other side, a great crowd gathered around him; and he was by the sea. ²²Then one of the leaders of the synagogue named Jairus came and, when he saw him, fell at his feet ²³and begged him repeatedly, 'My little daughter is at the point of death. Come and lay your hands on her, so that she may be made well, and live.' ²⁴So he went with him. And a large crowd followed him and pressed in on him. ²⁵Now there was a woman who had been suffering

from haemorrhages for twelve years. ²⁶She had endured much under many physicians, and had spent all that she had; and she was no better, but rather grew worse. ²⁷She had heard about Jesus, and came up behind him in the crowd and touched his cloak, ²⁸for she said, 'If I but touch his clothes, I will be made well.' ²⁹Immediately her haemorrhage stopped; and she felt in her body that she was healed of her disease. ³⁰Immediately aware that power had gone forth from him, Jesus turned about in the crowd and said, 'Who touched my clothes?' ³¹And his disciples said to him, 'You see the crowd pressing in on you; how can you say, "Who touched me?"' ³²He looked all around to see who had done it. ³³But the woman, knowing what had happened to her, came in fear and trembling, fell down before him, and told him the whole truth. ³⁴He said to her, 'Daughter, your faith has made you well; go in peace, and be healed of your disease.'

³⁵While he was still speaking, some people came from the leader's house to say, 'Your daughter is dead. Why trouble the teacher any further?' ³⁶But overhearing what they said, Jesus said to the leader of the synagogue, 'Do not fear, only believe.' ³⁷He allowed no one to follow him except Peter, James, and John, the brother of James. ³⁸When they came to the house of the leader of the synagogue, he saw a commotion, people weeping and wailing loudly. ³⁹When he had entered, he said to them, 'Why do you make a commotion and weep? The child is not dead but sleeping.' ⁴⁰And they laughed at him. Then he put them all outside, and took the child's father and mother and those who were with him, and went in where the child was. ⁴¹He took her by the hand and said to her, 'Talitha cum,' which means, 'Little girl, get up!' ⁴²And immediately the girl got up and began to walk about (she was twelve years of age). At this they were overcome with amazement. ⁴³He strictly ordered them that no one should know this, and told them to give her something to eat.

chapter **SIX**

The **Rejection** of Jesus at Nazareth

¹He left that place and came to his hometown, and his disciples followed him. ²On the sabbath he began to teach in the synagogue, and many who heard him were astounded. They said, 'Where did this man get all this? What is this wisdom that has been given to him? What deeds of power are being done by his hands! ³Is not this the carpenter, the son of Mary and brother of James and Joses and Judas and Simon, and are not his sisters here with us?' And they took offence at him. ⁴Then Jesus said to them, 'Prophets are not without honour, except in their hometown, and among their own kin, and in their own house.' ⁵And he could do no deed of power there, except that he laid his hands on a few sick people and cured them. ⁶And he was amazed at their unbelief.

APOSTOLIC JOURNEYS (6:6B–9:50)

The **Mission** of the Twelve

Then he went about among the villages teaching. ⁷He called the twelve and began to send them out two by two, and gave them authority over the unclean spirits. ⁸He ordered them to take nothing for their journey except a staff; no bread, no bag, no money in their belts; ⁹but to wear sandals and not to put on two tunics. ¹⁰He said to them, 'Wherever you enter a house, stay there until you leave the place. ¹¹If any place will not welcome you and they refuse to hear you, as you leave, shake off the dust that is on your feet as a testimony against them.' ¹²So they went out and proclaimed that all should repent. ¹³They cast out many demons, and anointed with oil many who were sick and cured them.

The **Death** of John the Baptist

¹⁴King Herod heard of it, for Jesus' name had become known. Some were saying, 'John the baptiser has been raised from the dead; and for this reason these powers are at work in him.' ¹⁵But others said, 'It is Elijah.' And others said, 'It is a prophet, like one of the prophets of old.' ¹⁶But when Herod heard of it, he said, 'John, whom I beheaded, has been raised.'

¹⁷For Herod himself had sent men who arrested John, bound him, and put him in prison on account of Herodias, his brother Philip's wife, because Herod had married her. ¹⁸For John had been telling Herod, 'It is not lawful for you to have your brother's wife.' ¹⁹And Herodias had a grudge against him, and wanted to kill him. But she could not, ²⁰for Herod feared John, knowing that he was a righteous and holy man, and he protected him. When he heard him, he was greatly perplexed; and yet he liked to listen to him. ²¹But an opportunity came when Herod on his birthday gave a banquet for his courtiers and officers and for the leaders of Galilee. ²²When his daughter Herodias came in and danced, she pleased Herod and his guests; and the king said to the girl, 'Ask me for whatever you wish, and I will give it.' ²³And he solemnly swore to her, 'Whatever you ask me, I will give you, even half of my kingdom.' ²⁴She went out and said to her mother, 'What should I ask for?' She replied, 'The head of John the baptiser.' ²⁵Immediately she rushed back to the king and requested, 'I want you to give me at once the head of John the Baptist on a platter.' ²⁶The king was deeply grieved; yet out of regard for his oaths and for the guests, he did not want to refuse her. ²⁷Immediately the king sent a soldier of the guard with orders to bring John's head. He went and beheaded him in the prison, ²⁸brought his head on a platter, and gave it to the girl. Then the girl gave it to her mother. ²⁹When his disciples heard about it, they came and took his body, and laid it in a tomb.

Feeding the Five Thousand

³⁰The apostles gathered around Jesus, and told him all that they had done and taught. ³¹He said to them, 'Come away to a deserted place all by yourselves and rest a while.' For many were coming and going, and they had no leisure even to eat. ³²And they went away in the boat to a deserted place by themselves. ³³Now many saw them going and recognised them, and they hurried there on foot from all the towns and arrived ahead of them. ³⁴As he went ashore, he saw a great crowd; and he had compassion for them, because they were like sheep without a shepherd; and he began to teach them many things. ³⁵When it grew late, his disciples came to him and said, 'This is a deserted place, and the hour is now very late; ³⁶send them away so that they may go into the surrounding country and villages and buy something for themselves to eat.' ³⁷But he answered them, 'You give them something to eat.' They said to him, 'Are we to go and buy two hundred denarii worth of bread, and give it to them to eat?' ³⁸And he said to them, 'How many loaves have you? Go and see.' When they had found out, they said, 'Five, and two fish.' ³⁹Then he ordered them to get all the people to sit down in groups on the green grass. ⁴⁰So they sat down in groups of hundreds and of fifties. ⁴¹Taking the five loaves and the two fish, he looked up to heaven, and blessed and broke the loaves, and gave them to his disciples to set before the people; and he divided the two fish among them all. ⁴²And all ate and were filled; ⁴³and they took up twelve baskets full of broken pieces and of the fish. ⁴⁴Those who had eaten the loaves numbered five thousand men.

Jesus Walks on Water

⁴⁵Immediately he made his disciples get into the boat and go on ahead to the other side, to Bethsaida, while he dismissed the crowd. ⁴⁶After saying farewell to them, he went up on the mountain to pray.

⁴⁷When evening came, the boat was out on the sea, and he was alone on the land. ⁴⁸When he saw that they were straining at the oars against an adverse wind, he came towards them early in the morning, walking on the sea. He intended to pass them by. ⁴⁹But when they saw him walking on the sea, they thought it was a ghost and cried out; ⁵⁰for they all saw him and were terrified. But immediately he spoke to them and said, 'Take heart, it is I; do not be afraid.' ⁵¹Then he got into the boat with them and the wind ceased. And they were utterly astounded, ⁵²for they did not understand about the loaves, but their hearts were hardened.

Healing the Sick
in Gennesaret

53When they had crossed over, they came to land at Gennesaret and moored the boat. 54When they got out of the boat, people at once recognised him, 55and rushed about that whole region and began to bring the sick on mats to wherever they heard he was. 56And wherever he went, into villages or cities or farms, they laid the sick in the marketplaces, and begged him that they might touch even the fringe of his cloak; and all who touched it were healed.

The Traditions of
the Elders

1Now when the Pharisees and some of the scribes who had come from Jerusalem gathered around him, 2they noticed that some of his disciples were eating with defiled hands, that is, without washing them. 3(For the Pharisees, and all the Jews, do not eat unless they thoroughly wash their hands, thus observing the tradition of the elders; 4and they do not eat anything from the market unless they wash it; and there are also many other traditions that they observe, the washing of cups, pots, and bronze kettles.) 5So the Pharisees and the scribes asked him, 'Why do your disciples not live according to the tradition of the elders, but eat with defiled hands?'

... and all who touched it were healed.

⁶He said to them, 'Isaiah prophesied rightly about you hypocrites, as it is written,
"This people honours me with their lips,
but their hearts are far from me;
⁷in vain do they worship me,
teaching human precepts as doctrines."
⁸You abandon the commandment of God and hold to human tradition.'
⁹Then he said to them, 'You have a fine way of rejecting the commandment of God in order to keep your tradition! ¹⁰For Moses said, "Honour your father and your mother"; and, "Whoever speaks evil of father or mother must surely die." ¹¹But you say that if anyone tells father or mother, "Whatever support you might have had from me is Corban" (that is, an offering to God) – ¹²then you no longer permit doing anything for a father or mother, ¹³thus making void the word of God through your tradition that you have handed on. And you do many things like this.'
¹⁴Then he called the crowd again and said to them, 'Listen to me, all of you, and understand: ¹⁵there is nothing outside a person that by going in can defile, but the things that come out are what defile.'
¹⁷When he had left the crowd and entered the house, his disciples asked him about the parable. ¹⁸He said to them, 'Then do you also fail to understand? Do you not see that whatever goes into a person from outside cannot defile, ¹⁹since

it enters, not the heart but the stomach, and goes out into the sewer?' (Thus he declared all foods clean.) ²⁰And he said, 'It is what comes out of a person that defiles. ²¹For it is from within, from the human heart, that evil intentions come: fornication, theft, murder, ²²adultery, avarice, wickedness, deceit, licentiousness, envy, slander, pride, folly. ²³All these evil things come from within, and they defile a person.'

The Syrophoenician Woman's Faith

24From there he set out and went away to the region of Tyre. He entered a house and did not want anyone to know he was there. Yet he could not escape notice, 25but a woman whose little daughter had an unclean spirit immediately heard about him, and she came and bowed down at his feet. 26Now the woman was a Gentile, of Syrophoenician origin. She begged him to cast the demon out of her daughter. 27He said to her, 'Let the children be fed first, for it is not fair to take the children's food and throw it to the dogs.' 28But she answered him, 'Sir, even the dogs under the table eat the children's crumbs.' 29Then he said to her, 'For saying that, you may go – the demon has left your daughter.' 30So she went home, found the child lying on the bed, and the demon gone.

Jesus Cures a Deaf Man

31Then he returned from the region of Tyre, and went by way of Sidon towards the Sea of Galilee, in the region of the Decapolis. 32They brought to him a deaf man who had an impediment in his speech; and they begged him to lay his hand on him. 33He took him aside in private, away from the crowd, and put his fingers into his ears, and he spat and touched his tongue. 34Then looking up to heaven, he sighed and said to him, 'Ephphatha,' that is, 'Be opened.' 35And immediately his ears were opened, his tongue was released, and he spoke plainly. 36Then Jesus ordered them to tell no one; but the more he ordered them, the more zealously they proclaimed it. 37They were astounded beyond measure, saying, 'He has done everything well; he even makes the deaf to hear and the mute to speak.'

chapter EIGHT

Feeding the Four Thousand

1In those days when there was again a great crowd without anything to eat, he called his disciples and said to them, 2'I have compassion for the crowd, because they have been with me now for three days and have nothing to eat. 3If I send them away hungry to their homes, they will faint on the way – and some of them have come from a great distance.' 4His disciples replied, 'How can one feed these people with bread here in the desert?' 5He asked them, 'How many loaves do you have?' They said, 'Seven.' 6Then he ordered the crowd to sit down on the ground; and he took the seven loaves, and after giving thanks he broke them and gave them to his disciples to distribute; and they distributed them to the crowd. 7They had also a few small fish; and after blessing them, he ordered that these too should be distributed. 8They ate and were filled; and they took up the broken pieces left over, seven baskets full. 9Now there were about four thousand people. And he sent them away. 10And immediately he got into the boat with his disciples and went to the district of Dalmanutha.

The Demand for a Sign

¹¹The Pharisees came and began to argue with him, asking him for a sign from heaven, to test him. ¹²And he sighed deeply in his spirit and said, 'Why does this generation ask for a sign? Truly I tell you, no sign will be given to this generation.' ¹³And he left them, and getting into the boat again, he went across to the other side.

The Yeast of the **Pharisees** and of **Herod**

¹⁴Now the disciples had forgotten to bring any bread; and they had only one loaf with them in the boat. ¹⁵And he cautioned them, saying, 'Watch out – beware of the yeast of the Pharisees and the yeast of Herod.' ¹⁶They said to one another, 'It is because we have no bread.' ¹⁷And becoming aware of it, Jesus said to them, 'Why are you talking about having no bread? Do you still not perceive or understand? Are your hearts hardened? ¹⁸Do you have eyes, and fail to see? Do you have ears, and fail to hear? And do you not remember? ¹⁹When I broke the five loaves for the five thousand, how many baskets full of broken pieces did you collect?' They said to him, 'Twelve.' ²⁰'And the seven for the four thousand, how many baskets full of broken pieces did you collect?' And they said to him, 'Seven.' ²¹Then he said to them, 'Do you not yet understand?'

Jesus Cures a Blind Man at Bethsaida

²²They came to Bethsaida. Some people brought a blind man to him and begged him to touch him. ²³He took the blind man by the hand and led him out of the village; and when he had put saliva on his eyes and laid his hands on him, he asked him, 'Can you see anything?' ²⁴And the man looked up and said, 'I can see people, but they look like trees, walking.' ²⁵Then Jesus laid his hands on his eyes again; and he looked intently and his sight was restored, and he saw everything clearly. ²⁶Then he sent him away to his home, saying, 'Do not even go into the village.'

Peter's Declaration about Jesus

²⁷Jesus went on with his disciples to the villages of Caesarea Philippi; and on the way he asked his disciples, 'Who do people say that I am?' ²⁸And they answered him, 'John the Baptist; and others, Elijah; and still others, one of the prophets.' ²⁹He asked them, 'But who do you say that I am?' Peter answered him, 'You are the Messiah.' ³⁰And he sternly ordered them not to tell anyone about him.

Jesus Foretells His Death and Resurrection

³¹Then he began to teach them that the Son of Man must undergo great suffering, and be rejected by the elders, the chief priests, and the scribes, and be killed, and after three days rise again. ³²He said all this quite openly. And Peter took him aside and began to rebuke him. ³³But turning and looking at his disciples, he rebuked Peter and said, 'Get behind me, Satan! For you are setting your mind not on divine things but on human things.'

³⁴He called the crowd with his disciples, and said to them, 'If any want to become my followers, let them deny themselves and take up their cross and follow me. ³⁵For those who want to save their life will lose it, and those who lose their life for my sake, and for the sake of the gospel, will save it. ³⁶For what will it profit them to gain the whole world and forfeit their life? ³⁷Indeed, what can they give in return for their life? ³⁸Those who are ashamed of me and of my words in this adulterous and sinful generation, of them the Son of Man will also be ashamed when he comes in the glory of his Father with the holy angels.'

chapter NINE

¹And he said to them, 'Truly I tell you, there are some standing here who will not taste death until they see that the kingdom of God has come with power.'

The **Transfiguration**

²Six days later, Jesus took with him Peter and James and John, and led them up a high mountain apart, by themselves. And he was transfigured before them, ³and his clothes became dazzling white, such as no one on earth could bleach them. ⁴And there appeared to them Elijah with Moses, who were talking with Jesus. ⁵Then Peter said to Jesus, 'Rabbi, it is good for us to be here; let us make three dwellings, one for you, one for Moses, and one for Elijah.' ⁶He did not know what to say, for they were terrified. ⁷Then a cloud overshadowed them, and from the cloud there came a voice, 'This is my Son, the Beloved; listen to him!' ⁸Suddenly when they looked around, they saw no one with them any more, but only Jesus.

The Coming of **Elijah**

⁹As they were coming down the mountain, he ordered them to tell no one about what they had seen, until after the Son of Man had risen from the dead. ¹⁰So they kept the matter to themselves, questioning what this rising from the dead could mean. ¹¹Then they asked him, 'Why do the scribes say that Elijah must come first?' ¹²He said to them, 'Elijah is indeed coming first to restore all things. How then is it written about the Son of Man, that he is to go through many sufferings and be treated with contempt? ¹³But I tell you that Elijah has come, and they did to him whatever they pleased, as it is written about him.'

The Healing of a Boy with a Spirit

[14]When they came to the disciples, they saw a great crowd around them, and some scribes arguing with them. [15]When the whole crowd saw him, they were immediately overcome with awe, and they ran forward to greet him. [16]He asked them, 'What are you arguing about with them?' [17]Someone from the crowd answered him, 'Teacher, I brought you my son; he has a spirit that makes him unable to speak; [18]and whenever it seizes him, it dashes him down; and he foams and grinds his teeth and becomes rigid; and I asked your disciples to cast it out, but they could not do so.' [19]He answered them, 'You faithless generation, how much longer must I be among you? How much longer must I put up with you? Bring him to me.' [20]And they brought the boy to him. When the spirit saw him, immediately it convulsed the boy, and he fell on the ground and rolled about, foaming at the mouth. [21]Jesus asked the father, 'How long has this been happening to him?' And he said, 'From childhood. [22]It has often cast him into the fire and into the water, to destroy him; but if you are able to do anything, have pity on us and help us.' [23]Jesus said to him, 'If you are able! – All things can be done for the one who believes.' [24]Immediately the father of the child cried out, 'I believe; help my unbelief!' [25]When Jesus saw that a crowd came running together, he rebuked the unclean spirit, saying to it, 'You spirit that keeps this boy from speaking and hearing, I command you, come out of him, and never enter him again!' [26]After crying out and convulsing him terribly, it came out, and the boy was like a corpse, so that most of them said, 'He is dead.' [27]But Jesus took him by the hand and lifted him up, and he was able to stand. [28]When he had entered the house, his disciples asked him privately, 'Why could we not cast it out?' [29]He said to them, 'This kind can come out only through prayer.'

'Whoever welcomes one such child in my name welcomes me ...'

Jesus Again **Foretells His Death** and **Resurrection**

³⁰They went on from there and passed through Galilee. He did not want anyone to know it; ³¹for he was teaching his disciples, saying to them, 'The Son of Man is to be betrayed into human hands, and they will kill him, and three days after being killed, he will rise again.' ³²But they did not understand what he was saying and were afraid to ask him.

Who Is the **Greatest**?

³³Then they came to Capernaum; and when he was in the house he asked them, 'What were you arguing about on the way?' ³⁴But they were silent, for on the way they had argued with one another who was the greatest. ³⁵He sat down, called the twelve, and said to them, 'Whoever wants to be first must be last of all and servant of all.' ³⁶Then he took a little child and put it among them; and taking it in his arms, he said to them, ³⁷'Whoever welcomes one such child in my name welcomes me, and whoever welcomes me welcomes not me but the one who sent me.'

Another **Exorcist**

³⁸John said to him, 'Teacher, we saw someone casting out demons in your name, and we tried to stop him, because he was not following us.' ³⁹But Jesus said, 'Do not stop him; for no one who does a deed of power in my name will be able soon afterward to speak evil of me. ⁴⁰Whoever is not against us is for us. ⁴¹For truly I tell you, whoever gives you a cup of water to drink because you bear the name of Christ will by no means lose the reward.

Temptations to Sin

⁴²'If any of you put a stumbling block before one of these little ones who believe in me, it would be better for you if a great millstone were hung around your neck and you were thrown into the sea. ⁴³If your hand causes you to stumble, cut it off; it is better for you to enter life maimed than to have two hands and to go to hell, to the unquenchable fire. ⁴⁵And if your foot causes you to stumble, cut it off; it is better for you to enter life lame than to have two feet and to be thrown into hell. ⁴⁷And if your eye causes you to stumble, tear it out; it is better for you to enter the kingdom of God with one eye than to have two eyes and to be thrown into hell, ⁴⁸ where their worm never dies, and the fire is never quenched. ⁴⁹'For everyone will be salted with fire. ⁵⁰Salt is good; but if salt has lost its saltiness, how can you season it? Have salt in yourselves, and be at peace with one another.'

chapter **TEN**

Teaching about **Divorce**

¹He left that place and went to the region of Judea and beyond the Jordan. And crowds again gathered around him; and, as was his custom, he again taught them.
²Some Pharisees came, and to test him they asked, 'Is it lawful for a man to divorce his wife?' ³He answered them, 'What did Moses command you?' ⁴They said, 'Moses allowed a man to write a certificate of dismissal and to divorce her.' ⁵But Jesus said to them, 'Because of your hardness of heart he wrote this commandment for you. ⁶But from the beginning of creation, "God made them male and female." ⁷"For this reason a man shall leave his father and mother and be joined to his wife, ⁸and the two shall become one flesh." So they are no longer two, but one flesh. ⁹Therefore what God has joined together, let no one separate.'
¹⁰Then in the house the disciples asked him again about this matter. ¹¹He said to them, 'Whoever divorces his wife and marries another commits adultery against her; ¹²and if she divorces her husband and marries another, she commits adultery.'

Jesus Blesses Little **Children**

¹³People were bringing little children to him in order that he might touch them; and the disciples spoke sternly to them. ¹⁴But when Jesus saw this, he was indignant and said to them, 'Let the little children come to me; do not stop them; for it is to such as these that the kingdom of God belongs. ¹⁵Truly I tell you, whoever does not receive the kingdom of God as a little child will never enter it.' ¹⁶And he took them up in his arms, laid his hands on them, and blessed them.

The **Rich Man**

17As he was setting out on a journey, a man ran up and knelt before him, and asked him, 'Good Teacher, what must I do to inherit eternal life?' 18Jesus said to him, 'Why do you call me good? No one is good but God alone. 19You know the commandments? "You shall not murder; You shall not commit adultery; You shall not steal; You shall not bear false witness; you shall not defraud; Honour your father and mother."' 20He said to him, 'Teacher, I have kept all these since my youth.' 21Jesus, looking at him, loved him and said, 'You lack one thing; go, sell what you own, and give the money to the poor, and you will have treasure in heaven; then come, follow me.' 22When he heard this, he was shocked and went away grieving, for he had many possessions.
23Then Jesus looked around and said to his disciples, 'How hard it will be for those who have wealth to enter the kingdom of God!' 24And the disciples were perplexed at these words. But Jesus said to them again, 'Children, how hard it is to enter the kingdom of God! 25It is easier for a camel to go through the eye of a needle than for someone who is rich to enter the kingdom of God.' 26They were greatly astounded and said to one another, 'Then who can be saved?' 27Jesus looked at them and said, 'For mortals it is impossible, but not for God; for God all things are possible.'
28Peter began to say to him, 'Look, we have left everything and followed you.' 29Jesus said, 'Truly I tell you, there is no one who has left house or brothers or sisters or mother or father or children or fields, for my sake and for the sake of the good news, 30who will not receive a hundredfold now in this age – houses, brothers and sisters, mothers and children, and fields with persecutions – and in the age to come eternal life. 31But many who are first will be last, and the last will be first.'

A Third Time Jesus Foretells His Death and Resurrection

32They were on the road, going up to Jerusalem, and Jesus was walking ahead of them; they were amazed, and those who followed were afraid. He took the twelve aside again and began to tell them what was to happen to him, 33saying, 'See, we are going up to Jerusalem, and the Son of Man will be handed over to the chief priests and the scribes, and they will condemn him to death; then they will hand him over to the Gentiles; 34they will mock him, and spit upon him, and flog him, and kill him; and after three days he will rise again.'

The Request of James and John

35James and John, the sons of Zebedee, came forward to him and said to him, 'Teacher, we want you to do for us whatever we ask of you.' 36And he said to them, 'What is it you want me to do for you?' 37And they said to him, 'Grant us to sit, one at your right hand and one at your left, in your glory.' 38But Jesus said to them, 'You do not know what you are asking. Are you able to drink the cup that I drink, or be baptised with the baptism that I am baptised with?' 39They replied, 'We are able.' Then Jesus said to them, 'The cup that I drink you will drink; and with the baptism with which I am baptised, you will be baptised; 40but to sit at my right hand or at my left is not mine to grant, but it is for those for whom it has been prepared.' 41When the ten heard this, they began to be angry with James and John. 42So Jesus called them and said to them, 'You know that among the Gentiles those whom they recognise as their rulers lord it over them, and their great ones are tyrants over them. 43But it is not so among you; but whoever wishes to become great among you must be your servant, 44and whoever wishes to be first among you must be slave of all. 45For the Son of Man came not to be served but to serve, and to give his life a ransom for many.'

The Healing of Blind Bartimaeus

46They came to Jericho. As he and his disciples and a large crowd were leaving Jericho, Bartimaeus son of Timaeus, a blind beggar, was sitting by the roadside. 47When he heard that it was Jesus of Nazareth, he began to shout out and say, 'Jesus, Son of David, have mercy on me!' 48Many sternly ordered him to be quiet, but he cried out even more loudly, 'Son of David, have mercy on me!' 49Jesus stood still and said, 'Call him here.' And they called the blind man, saying to him, 'Take heart; get up, he is calling you.' 50So throwing off his cloak, he sprang up and came to Jesus. 51Then Jesus said to him, 'What do you want me to do for you?' The blind man said to him, 'My teacher, let me see again.' 52Jesus said to him, 'Go; your faith has made you well.' Immediately he regained his sight and followed him on the way.

MINISTRY AND PASSION IN JERUSALEM (11:1–16:20)

chapter ELEVEN

Jesus' Triumphal Entry into Jerusalem

[1]When they were approaching Jerusalem, at Bethphage and Bethany, near the Mount of Olives, he sent two of his disciples [2]and said to them, 'Go into the village ahead of you, and immediately as you enter it, you will find tied there a colt that has never been ridden; untie it and bring it. [3]If anyone says to you, "Why are you doing this?" just say this, "The Lord needs it and will send it back here immediately."' [4]They went away and found a colt tied near a door, outside in the street. As they were untying it, [5]some of the bystanders said to them, 'What are you doing, untying the colt?' [6]They told them what Jesus had said; and they allowed them to take it. [7]Then they brought the colt to Jesus and threw their cloaks on it; and he sat on it. [8]Many people spread their cloaks on the road, and others spread leafy branches that they had cut in the fields. [9]Then those who went ahead and those who followed were shouting,

'Hosanna!
Blessed is the one who comes
in the name of the Lord!
[10]Blessed is the coming kingdom
of our ancestor David!
Hosanna in the highest heaven!'

[11]Then he entered Jerusalem and went into the temple; and when he had looked around at everything, as it was already late, he went out to Bethany with the twelve.

Jesus Curses the Fig Tree

¹²On the following day, when they came from Bethany, he was hungry. ¹³Seeing in the distance a fig tree in leaf, he went to see whether perhaps he would find anything on it. When he came to it, he found nothing but leaves, for it was not the season for figs. ¹⁴He said to it, 'May no one ever eat fruit from you again.' And his disciples heard it.

Jesus Cleanses the Temple

¹⁵Then they came to Jerusalem. And he entered the temple and began to drive out those who were selling and those who were buying in the temple, and he overturned the tables of the money changers and the seats of those who sold doves; ¹⁶and he would not allow anyone to carry anything through the temple. ¹⁷He was teaching and saying, 'Is it not written,
"My house shall be called a
house of prayer for all the nations"?
But you have made it a den of robbers.'
¹⁸And when the chief priests and the scribes heard it, they kept looking for a way to kill him; for they were afraid of him, because the whole crowd was spellbound by this teaching. ¹⁹And when evening came, Jesus and his disciples went out of the city.

The Lesson from the Withered Fig Tree

²⁰In the morning as they passed by, they saw the fig tree withered away to its roots. ²¹Then Peter remembered and said to him, 'Rabbi, look! The fig tree that you cursed has withered.' ²²Jesus answered them, 'Have faith in God. ²³Truly I tell you, if you say to this mountain, "Be taken up and thrown into the sea," and if you do not doubt in your heart, but believe that what you say will come to pass, it will be done for you. ²⁴So I tell you, whatever you ask for in prayer, believe that you have received it, and it will be yours.
²⁵'Whenever you stand praying, forgive, if you have anything against anyone; so that your Father in heaven may also forgive you your trespasses.'

Jesus' Authority is Questioned

27Again they came to Jerusalem. As he was walking in the temple, the chief priests, the scribes, and the elders came to him 28and said, 'By what authority are you doing these things? Who gave you this authority to do them?' 29Jesus said to them, 'I will ask you one question; answer me, and I will tell you by what authority I do these things. 30Did the baptism of John come from heaven, or was it of human origin? Answer me.' 31They argued with one another, 'If we say, "From heaven," he will say, "Why then did you not believe him?" 32But shall we say, "Of human origin"?' – they were afraid of the crowd, for all regarded John as truly a prophet. 33So they answered Jesus, 'We do not know.' And Jesus said to them, 'Neither will I tell you by what authority I am doing these things.'

chapter TWELVE

The Parable of the Wicked Tenants

1Then he began to speak to them in parables. 'A man planted a vineyard, put a fence around it, dug a pit for the wine press, and built a watchtower; then he leased it to tenants and went to another country. 2When the season came, he sent a slave to the tenants to collect from them his share of the produce of the vineyard. 3But they seized him, and beat him, and sent him away empty-handed. 4And again he sent another slave to them; this one they beat over the head and insulted. 5Then he sent another, and that one they killed. And so it was with many others; some they beat, and others they killed. 6He had still one other, a beloved son. Finally he sent him to them, saying, 'They will respect my son.' 7But those tenants said to one another, 'This is the heir; come, let us kill him, and the inheritance will be ours.' 8So they seized him, killed him, and threw him out of the vineyard. 9What then will the owner of the vineyard do? He will come and destroy the tenants and give the vineyard to others. 10Have you not read this scripture:
"The stone that the builders rejected
has become the cornerstone;
11this was the Lord's doing,
and it is amazing in our eyes?'"
12When they realised that he had told this parable against them, they wanted to arrest him, but they feared the crowd. So they left him and went away.

'The stone that the builders rejected
has become the cornerstone ...'

The Question about Paying Taxes

¹³Then they sent to him some Pharisees and some Herodians to trap him in what he said. ¹⁴And they came and said to him, 'Teacher, we know that you are sincere, and show deference to no one; for you do not regard people with partiality, but teach the way of God in accordance with truth. Is it lawful to pay taxes to the emperor, or not? ¹⁵Should we pay them, or should we not?' But knowing their hypocrisy, he said to them, 'Why are you putting me to the test? Bring me a denarius and let me see it.' ¹⁶And they brought one. Then he said to them, 'Whose head is this, and whose title?' They answered, 'The emperor's.' ¹⁷Jesus said to them, 'Give to the emperor the things that are the emperor's, and to God the things that are God's.' And they were utterly amazed at him.

The Question about the Resurrection

¹⁸Some Sadducees, who say there is no resurrection, came to him and asked him a question, saying, ¹⁹'Teacher, Moses wrote for us that "if a man's brother dies, leaving a wife but no child, the man shall marry the widow and raise up children for his brother." ²⁰There were seven brothers; the first married and, when he died, left no children; ²¹and the second married her and died, leaving no children; and the third likewise; ²²none of the seven left children. Last of all the woman herself died. ²³In the resurrection whose wife will she be? For the seven had married her.' ²⁴Jesus said to them, 'Is not this the reason you are wrong, that you know neither the scriptures nor the power of God? ²⁵For when they rise from the dead, they neither marry nor are given in marriage, but are like angels in heaven. ²⁶And as for the dead being raised, have you not read in the book of Moses, in the story about the bush, how God said to him, "I am the God of Abraham, the God of Isaac, and the God of Jacob"? ²⁷He is God not of the dead, but of the living; you are quite wrong.'

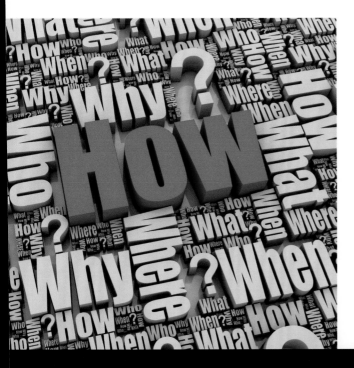

The First Commandment

²⁸One of the scribes came near and heard them disputing with one another, and seeing that he answered them well, he asked him, 'Which commandment is the first of all?' ²⁹Jesus answered, 'The first is, "Hear, O Israel: the Lord our God, the Lord is one; ³⁰you shall love the Lord your God with all your heart, and with all your soul, and with all your mind, and with all your strength." ³¹The second is this, "You shall love your neighbour as yourself." There is no other commandment greater than these.' ³²Then the scribe said to him, 'You are right, Teacher; you have truly said that "he is one, and besides him there is no other"; ³³and "to love him with all the heart, and with all the understanding, and with all the strength," and "to love one's neighbour as oneself," – this is much more important than all whole burnt offerings and sacrifices.' ³⁴When Jesus saw that he answered wisely, he said to him, 'You are not far from the kingdom of God.' After that no one dared to ask him any question.

The Question about David's Son

35While Jesus was teaching in the temple, he said, 'How can the scribes say that the Messiah is the son of David? 36David himself, by the Holy Spirit, declared,
"The Lord said to my Lord,
'Sit at my right hand,
until I put your enemies under your feet.'"
37David himself calls him Lord; so how can he be his son?' And the large crowd was listening to him with delight.

Jesus Denounces the Scribes

38As he taught, he said, 'Beware of the scribes, who like to walk around in long robes, and to be greeted with respect in the marketplaces, 39and to have the best seats in the synagogues and places of honour at banquets! 40They devour widows' houses and for the sake of appearance say long prayers. They will receive the greater condemnation.'

The Widow's Offering

41He sat down opposite the treasury, and watched the crowd putting money into the treasury. Many rich people put in large sums. 42A poor widow came and put in two small copper coins, which are worth a penny. 43Then he called his disciples and said to them, 'Truly I tell you, this poor widow has put in more than all those who are contributing to the treasury. 44For all of them have contributed out of their abundance; but she out of her poverty has put in everything she had, all she had to live on.'

chapter THIRTEEN

The **Destruction** of the Temple **Foretold**

¹As he came out of the temple, one of his disciples said to him, 'Look, Teacher, what large stones and what large buildings!' ²Then Jesus asked him, 'Do you see these great buildings? Not one stone will be left here upon another; all will be thrown down.'

³When he was sitting on the Mount of Olives opposite the temple, Peter, James, John, and Andrew asked him privately, ⁴'Tell us, when will this be, and what will be the sign that all these things are about to be accomplished?' ⁵Then Jesus began to say to them, 'Beware that no one leads you astray. ⁶Many will come in my name and say, "I am he!" and they will lead many astray. ⁷When you hear of wars and rumours of wars, do not be alarmed; this must take place, but the end is still to come. ⁸For nation will rise against nation, and kingdom against kingdom; there will be earthquakes in various places; there will be famines. This is but the beginning of the birthpangs.

Persecution Foretold

⁹'As for yourselves, beware; for they will hand you over to councils; and you will be beaten in synagogues; and you will stand before governors and kings because of me, as a testimony to them. ¹⁰And the good news must first be proclaimed to all nations. ¹¹When they bring you to trial and hand you over, do not worry beforehand about what you are to say; but say whatever is given you at that time, for it is not you who speak, but the Holy Spirit. ¹²Brother will betray brother to death, and a father his child, and children will rise against parents and have them put to death; ¹³and you will be hated by all because of my name. But the one who endures to the end will be saved.

The **Desolating Sacrilege**

14'But when you see the desolating sacrilege set up where it ought not to be (let the reader understand), then those in Judea must flee to the mountains; 15the one on the housetop must not go down or enter the house to take anything away; 16the one in the field must not turn back to get a coat. 17Woe to those who are pregnant and to those who are nursing infants in those days! 18Pray that it may not be in winter. 19For in those days there will be suffering, such as has not been from the beginning of the creation that God created until now, no, and never will be. 20And if the Lord had not cut short those days, no one would be saved; but for the sake of the elect, whom he chose, he has cut short those days. 21And if anyone says to you at that time, "Look! Here is the Messiah!" or "Look! There he is!" – do not believe it. 22False messiahs and false prophets will appear and produce signs and omens, to lead astray, if possible, the elect. 23But be alert; I have already told you everything.

The **Coming** of the **Son of Man**

24'But in those days, after that suffering,
the sun will be darkened,
and the moon will not give its light,
25and the stars will be falling from heaven,
and the powers in the heavens will be shaken. 26Then they will see "the Son of Man coming in clouds" with great power and glory. 27Then he will send out the angels, and gather his elect from the four winds, from the ends of the earth to the ends of heaven.

'But the one who endures to the end will be saved.'

The Lesson of the Fig Tree

²⁸'From the fig tree learn its lesson: as soon as its branch becomes tender and puts forth its leaves, you know that summer is near. ²⁹So also, when you see these things taking place, you know that he is near, at the very gates. ³⁰Truly I tell you, this generation will not pass away until all these things have taken place. ³¹Heaven and earth will pass away, but my words will not pass away.'

The Necessity for Watchfulness

³²'But about that day or hour no one knows, neither the angels in heaven, nor the Son, but only the Father. ³³Beware, keep alert; for you do not know when the time will come. ³⁴It is like a man going on a journey, when he leaves home and puts his slaves in charge, each with his work, and commands the doorkeeper to be on the watch. ³⁵Therefore, keep awake – for you do not know when the master of the house will come, in the evening, or at midnight, or at cockcrow, or at dawn, ³⁶or else he may find you asleep when he comes suddenly. ³⁷And what I say to you I say to all: Keep awake.'

'Heaven and earth will pass away, but my words will not pass away.'

chapter **FOURTEEN**

The Plot to Kill Jesus

¹It was two days before the Passover and the festival of Unleavened Bread. The chief priests and the scribes were looking for a way to arrest Jesus by stealth and kill him; ²for they said, 'Not during the festival, or there may be a riot among the people.'

The Anointing at Bethany

³While he was at Bethany in the house of Simon the leper, as he sat at the table, a woman came with an alabaster jar of very costly ointment of nard, and she broke open the jar and poured the ointment on his head. ⁴But some were there who said to one another in anger, 'Why was the ointment wasted in this way? ⁵For this ointment could have been sold for more than three hundred denarii, and the money given to the poor.' And they scolded her. ⁶But Jesus said, 'Let her alone; why do you trouble her? She has performed a good service for me. ⁷For you always have the poor with you, and you can show kindness to them whenever you wish; but you will not always have me. ⁸She has done what she could; she has anointed my body beforehand for its burial. ⁹Truly I tell you, wherever the good news is proclaimed in the whole world, what she has done will be told in remembrance of her.'

Judas Agrees to Betray Jesus

¹⁰Then Judas Iscariot, who was one of the twelve, went to the chief priests in order to betray him to them. ¹¹When they heard it, they were greatly pleased, and promised to give him money. So he began to look for an opportunity to betray him.

The **Passover with** the **Disciples**

¹²On the first day of Unleavened Bread, when the Passover lamb is sacrificed, his disciples said to him, 'Where do you want us to go and make the preparations for you to eat the Passover?' ¹³So he sent two of his disciples, saying to them, 'Go into the city, and a man carrying a jar of water will meet you; follow him, ¹⁴and wherever he enters, say to the owner of the house, "The Teacher asks, Where is my guest room where I may eat the Passover with my disciples?" ¹⁵He will show you a large room upstairs, furnished and ready. Make preparations for us there.' ¹⁶So the disciples set out and went to the city, and found everything as he had told them; and they prepared the Passover meal.

¹⁷When it was evening, he came with the twelve. ¹⁸And when they had taken their places and were eating, Jesus said, 'Truly I tell you, one of you will betray me, one who is eating with me.' ¹⁹They began to be distressed and to say to him one after another, 'Surely, not I?' ²⁰He said to them, 'It is one of the twelve, one who is dipping bread into the bowl with me. ²¹For the Son of Man goes as it is written of him, but woe to that one by whom the Son of Man is betrayed! It would have been better for that one not to have been born.'

The Institution of **the Lord's Supper**

²²While they were eating, he took a loaf of bread, and after blessing it he broke it, gave it to them, and said, 'Take; this is my body.' ²³Then he took a cup, and after giving thanks he gave it to them, and all of them drank from it. ²⁴He said to them, 'This is my blood of the covenant, which is poured out for many. ²⁵Truly I tell you, I will never again drink of the fruit of the vine until that day when I drink it new in the kingdom of God.'

Peter's Denial Foretold

²⁶When they had sung the hymn, they went out to the Mount of Olives. ²⁷And Jesus said to them, 'You will all become deserters; for it is written,
"I will strike the shepherd,
and the sheep will be scattered."
²⁸But after I am raised up, I will go before you to Galilee.' ²⁹Peter said to him, 'Even though all become deserters, I will not.' ³⁰Jesus said to him, 'Truly I tell you, this day, this very night, before the cock crows twice, you will deny me three times.' ³¹But he said vehemently, 'Even though I must die with you, I will not deny you.' And all of them said the same.

Jesus Prays in Gethsemane

³²They went to a place called Gethsemane; and he said to his disciples, 'Sit here while I pray.' ³³He took with him Peter and James and John, and began to be distressed and agitated. ³⁴And he said to them, 'I am deeply grieved, even to death; remain here, and keep awake.' ³⁵And going a little farther, he threw himself on the ground and prayed that, if it were possible, the hour might pass from him. ³⁶He said, 'Abba, Father, for you all things are possible; remove this cup from me; yet, not what I want, but what you want.' ³⁷He came and found them sleeping; and he said to Peter, 'Simon, are you asleep? Could you not keep awake one hour? ³⁸Keep awake and pray that you may not come into the time of trial; the spirit indeed is willing, but the flesh is weak.' ³⁹And again he went away and prayed, saying the same words. ⁴⁰And once more he came and found them sleeping, for their eyes were very heavy; and they did not know what to say to him. ⁴¹He came a third time and said to them, 'Are you still sleeping and taking your rest? Enough! The hour has come; the Son of Man is betrayed into the hands of sinners. ⁴²Get up, let us be going. See, my betrayer is at hand.'

me. But let the scriptures be fulfilled.' 50All of them deserted him and fled.

51A certain young man was following him, wearing nothing but a linen cloth. They caught hold of him, 52but he left the linen cloth and ran off naked.

Jesus before the Council

53They took Jesus to the high priest; and all the chief priests, the elders, and the scribes were assembled. 54Peter had followed him at a distance, right into the courtyard of the high priest; and he was sitting with the guards, warming himself at the fire. 55Now the chief priests and the whole council were looking for testimony against Jesus to put him to death; but they found none. 56For many gave false testimony against him, and their testimony did not agree. 57Some stood up and gave false testimony against him, saying, 58'We heard him say, "I will destroy this temple that is made with hands, and in three days I will build another, not made with hands."' 59But even on this point their testimony did not agree. 60Then the high priest stood up before them and asked Jesus, 'Have you no answer? What is it that they testify against you?' 61But he was silent and did not answer. Again the high priest asked him, 'Are you the Messiah, the Son of the Blessed One?' 62Jesus said, 'I am; and

"you will see the Son of Man
seated at the right hand of the Power,"
and "coming with the clouds of heaven."'

63Then the high priest tore his clothes and said, 'Why do we still need witnesses? 64You have heard his blasphemy! What is your decision?' All of them condemned him as deserving death. 65Some began to spit on him, to blindfold him, and to strike him, saying to him, 'Prophesy!' The guards also took him over and beat him.

The Betrayal and Arrest of Jesus

43Immediately, while he was still speaking, Judas, one of the twelve, arrived; and with him there was a crowd with swords and clubs, from the chief priests, the scribes, and the elders. 44Now the betrayer had given them a sign, saying, 'The one I will kiss is the man; arrest him and lead him away under guard.' 45So when he came, he went up to him at once and said, 'Rabbi!' and kissed him. 46Then they laid hands on him and arrested him. 47But one of those who stood near drew his sword and struck the slave of the high priest, cutting off his ear. 48Then Jesus said to them, 'Have you come out with swords and clubs to arrest me as though I were a bandit? 49Day after day I was with you in the temple teaching, and you did not arrest

Peter Denies Jesus

[66]While Peter was below in the courtyard, one of the servant-girls of the high priest came by. [67]When she saw Peter warming himself, she stared at him and said, 'You also were with Jesus, the man from Nazareth.' [68]But he denied it, saying, 'I do not know or understand what you are talking about.' And he went out into the forecourt. Then the cock crowed. [69]And the servant-girl, on seeing him, began again to say to the bystanders, 'This man is one of them.' [70]But again he denied it.

Then after a little while the bystanders again said to Peter, 'Certainly you are one of them; for you are a Galilean.' [71]But he began to curse, and he swore an oath, 'I do not know this man you are talking about.' [72]At that moment the cock crowed for the second time. Then Peter remembered that Jesus had said to him, 'Before the cock crows twice, you will deny me three times.' And he broke down and wept.

chapter FIFTEEN

Jesus before **Pilate**

[1]As soon as it was morning, the chief priests held a consultation with the elders and scribes and the whole council. They bound Jesus, led him away, and handed him over to Pilate. [2]Pilate asked him, 'Are you the King of the Jews?' He answered him, 'You say so.' [3]Then the chief priests accused him of many things. [4]Pilate asked him again, 'Have you no answer? See how many charges they bring against you.' [5]But Jesus made no further reply, so that Pilate was amazed.

Pilate Hands **Jesus** over to Be Crucified

[6]Now at the festival he used to release a prisoner for them, anyone for whom they asked. [7]Now a man called Barabbas was in prison with the rebels who had committed murder during the insurrection. [8]So the crowd came and began to ask Pilate to do for them according to his custom. [9]Then he answered them, 'Do you want me to release for you the King of the Jews?' [10]For he realised that it was out of jealousy that the chief priests had handed him over. [11]But the chief priests stirred up the crowd to have him release Barabbas for them instead. [12]Pilate spoke to them again, 'Then what do you wish me to do with the man you call the King of the Jews?' [13]They shouted back, 'Crucify him!' [14]Pilate asked them, 'Why, what evil has he done?' But they shouted all the more, 'Crucify him!' [15]So Pilate, wishing to satisfy the crowd, released Barabbas for them; and after flogging Jesus, he handed him over to be crucified.

The Soldiers **Mock** Jesus

[16]Then the soldiers led him into the courtyard of the palace (that is, the governor's headquarters); and they called together the whole cohort. [17]And they clothed him in a purple cloak; and after twisting some thorns into a crown, they put it on him. [18]And they began saluting him, 'Hail, King of the Jews!' [19]They struck his head with a reed, spat upon him, and knelt down in homage to him. [20]After mocking him, they stripped him of the purple cloak and put his own clothes on him. Then they led him out to crucify him.

The Crucifixion of Jesus

[21]They compelled a passer-by, who was coming in from the country, to carry his cross; it was Simon of Cyrene, the father of Alexander and Rufus. [22]Then they brought Jesus to the place called Golgotha (which means the place of a skull). [23]And they offered him wine mixed with myrrh; but he did not take it. [24]And they crucified him, and divided his clothes among them, casting lots to decide what each should take.

[25]It was nine o'clock in the morning when they crucified him. [26]The inscription of the charge against him read, 'The King of the Jews.' [27]And with him they crucified two bandits, one on his right and one on his left. [29]Those who passed by derided him, shaking their heads and saying, 'Aha! You who would destroy the temple and build it in three days, [30]save yourself, and come down from the cross!' [31]In the same way the chief priests, along with the scribes, were also mocking him among themselves and saying, 'He saved others; he cannot save himself. [32]Let the Messiah, the King of Israel, come down from the cross now, so that we may see and believe.' Those who were crucified with him also taunted him.

The **Burial of Jesus**

42When evening had come, and since it was the day of Preparation, that is, the day before the sabbath, 43Joseph of Arimathea, a respected member of the council, who was also himself waiting expectantly for the kingdom of God, went boldly to Pilate and asked for the body of Jesus. 44Then Pilate wondered if he were already dead; and summoning the centurion, he asked him whether he had been dead for some time. 45When he learned from the centurion that he was dead, he granted the body to Joseph. 46Then Joseph bought a linen cloth, and taking down the body, wrapped it in the linen cloth, and laid it in a tomb that had been hewn out of the rock. He then rolled a stone against the door of the tomb. 47Mary Magdalene and Mary the mother of Joses saw where the body was laid.

The **Death of Jesus**

33When it was noon, darkness came over the whole land until three in the afternoon. 34At three o'clock Jesus cried out with a loud voice, 'Eloi, Eloi, lema sabachthani?' which means, 'My God, my God, why have you forsaken me?' 35When some of the bystanders heard it, they said, 'Listen, he is calling for Elijah.' 36And someone ran, filled a sponge with sour wine, put it on a stick, and gave it to him to drink, saying, 'Wait, let us see whether Elijah will come to take him down.' 37Then Jesus gave a loud cry and breathed his last. 38And the curtain of the temple was torn in two, from top to bottom. 39Now when the centurion, who stood facing him, saw that in this way he breathed his last, he said, 'Truly this man was God's Son!' 40There were also women looking on from a distance; among them were Mary Magdalene, and Mary the mother of James the younger and of Joses, and Salome. 41These used to follow him and provided for him when he was in Galilee; and there were many other women who had come up with him to Jerusalem.

chapter SIXTEEN

The **Resurrection of Jesus**

[1] When the sabbath was over, Mary Magdalene, and Mary the mother of James, and Salome bought spices, so that they might go and anoint him. [2] And very early on the first day of the week, when the sun had risen, they went to the tomb. [3] They had been saying to one another, 'Who will roll away the stone for us from the entrance to the tomb?' [4] When they looked up, they saw that the stone, which was very large, had already been rolled back. [5] As they entered the tomb, they saw a young man, dressed in a white robe, sitting on the right side; and they were alarmed. [6] But he said to them, 'Do not be alarmed; you are looking for Jesus of Nazareth, who was crucified. He has been raised; he is not here. Look, there is the place they laid him. [7] But go, tell his disciples and Peter that he is going ahead of you to Galilee; there you will see him, just as he told you.' [8] So they went out and fled from the tomb, for terror and amazement had seized them; and they said nothing to anyone, for they were afraid.

Jesus Appears to **Mary Magdalene**

[9] Now after he rose early on the first day of the week, he appeared first to Mary Magdalene, from whom he had cast out seven demons. [10] She went out and told those who had been with him, while they were mourning and weeping. [11] But when they heard that he was alive and had been seen by her, they would not believe it.

Jesus **Appears** to Two Disciples

¹²After this he appeared in another form to two of them, as they were walking into the country. ¹³And they went back and told the rest, but they did not believe them.

Jesus **Commissions** the **Disciples**

¹⁴Later he appeared to the eleven themselves as they were sitting at the table; and he upbraided them for their lack of faith and stubbornness, because they had not believed those who saw him after he had risen. ¹⁵And he said to them, 'Go into all the world and proclaim the good news to the whole creation. ¹⁶The one who believes and is baptised will be saved; but the one who does not believe will be condemned. ¹⁷And these signs will accompany those who believe: by using my name they will cast out demons; they will speak in new tongues; ¹⁸they will pick up snakes in their hands, and if they drink any deadly thing, it will not hurt them; they will lay their hands on the sick, and they will recover.'

The **Ascension** of Jesus

¹⁹So then the Lord Jesus, after he had spoken to them, was taken up into heaven and sat down at the right hand of God. ²⁰And they went out and proclaimed the good news everywhere, while the Lord worked with them and confirmed the message by the signs that accompanied it.

Lectio divina

Lectio divina (meaning 'divine reading' or 'holy reading') is an ancient method of paying attention to God's Word in Scripture in order to achieve a fuller understanding of the message and thus be better able to take it to heart in daily life. It was first practiced in the early Christian monasteries. Pope Benedict XVI said: 'I would like in particular to recall and recommend the ancient tradition of *lectio divina*: the diligent reading of Sacred Scripture accompanied by prayer brings about that intimate dialogue in which the person reading hears God who is speaking, and, in praying, responds with trusting openness of heart.'

Lectio divina is a particularly simple approach to prayer. It can be used individually or in groups. Ideally, you should choose the same time each day for this exercise and in a place free of distraction so that a daily habit will be learned.

So, choose a text of Scripture, something fairly brief and engaging. Then:

Lectio (read): Slowly read the text, being alert for God's Word to your life; notice what stands out for you or seems significant.

Meditatio (meditate): Read the text again. Pause and talk to God about what you are hearing. Meditation is like talking to God.

Contemplatio (contemplate): Read again. Now listen to and receive what God may be saying to you. Contemplation is like listening to God.

Oratio (pray): Recognise and pray whatever may be the deep desire of your heart.

Then some traditions add:

Actio (action): What does this study and prayer time call you to do? How will you take it to heart in your life now?

People from all walks of life are realising the benefits of this type of spiritual exercise. *Lectio divina* allows you to explore the deep wisdom of Scripture and to experience God in a very personal way.

Mark

Index

Chapter One

The Proclamation of John the Baptist (1:1-8)	9
The Baptism of Jesus (1:9-11)	9
The Temptation of Jesus (1:12-13)	9
The Beginning of the Galilean Ministry (1:14-15)	10
Jesus calls the First Disciples (1:16-20)	10
The Man with an Unclean Spirit (1:21-28)	11
Jesus Heals Many at Simon's House (1:29-34)	11
A Preaching Tour in Galilee (1:35-39)	12
Jesus Cleanses a Leper (1:40-45)	12

Chapter Two

Jesus Heals a Paralytic (2:1-12)	12
Jesus Calls Levi (2:13-17)	13
The Question about Fasting (2:18-22)	14
Pronouncement about the Sabbath (2:23-28)	14

Chapter Three

The Man with a Withered Hand (3:1-6)	15
A Multitude at the Seaside (3:7-12)	15
Jesus Appoints the Twelve (3:13-19)	17
Jesus and Beelzebul (3:20-30)	17
The True Kindred of Jesus (3:31-35)	17

Chapter Four

The Parable of the Sower (4:1-9)	18
The Purpose of the Parables (4:10-20)	19
A Lamp under a Bushel Basket (4:21-25)	19
The Parable of the Growing Seed (4:26-29)	20
The Parable of the Mustard Seed (4:30-32)	20
The Use of Parables (4:33-34)	20
Jesus Stills a Storm (4:35-41)	21

Chapter Five

Jesus Heals the Gerasene Demoniac (5:1-20)	22
A Girl Restored to Life and a Woman Healed (5:21-43)	22

Chapter Six

The Rejection of Jesus at Nazareth (6:1-6a)	25
The Mission of the Twelve (6:6b-13)	25
The Death of John the Baptist (6:14-29)	25
Feeding the Five Thousand (6:30-44)	26
Jesus Walks on Water (6:45-52)	27
Healing the Sick in Gennesaret (6:53-56)	28

Chapter Seven

The Traditions of the Elders (7:1-23)	28
The Syrophoenician Woman's Faith (7:24-30)	30
Jesus Cures a Deaf Man (7:31-37)	30

Chapter Eight

Feeding the Four Thousand (8:1-10)	30
The Demand for a Sign (8:11-13)	31
The Yeast of the Pharisees and of Herod (8:14-21)	31
Jesus Cures a Blind Man at Bethsaida (8:22-26)	31
Peter's Declaration about Jesus (8:27-30)	32
Jesus Foretells His Death and Resurrection (8:31–9:1)	32

Chapter Nine

The Transfiguration (9:2-8)	33
The Coming of Elijah (9:9-13)	33
The Healing of a Boy with a Spirit (9:14-29)	34
Jesus Again Foretells His Death and Resurrection (9:30-32)	35
Who Is the Greatest? (9:33-37)	35
Another Exorcist (9:38-41)	35
Temptations to Sin (9:42-50)	35

Chapter Ten

Teaching about Divorce (10:1-12)	36
Jesus Blesses Little Children (10:13-16)	36
The Rich Man (10:17-31)	38
A Third Time Jesus Foretells His Death and Resurrection (10:32-34)	39
The Request of James and John (10:35-45)	39
The Healing of Blind Bartimaeus (10:46-52)	39

Chapter Eleven

Jesus' Triumphal Entry into Jerusalem (11:1-11)   40
Jesus Curses the Fig Tree (11:12-14)   41
Jesus Cleanses the Temple (11:15-19)   41
The Lesson from the Withered Fig Tree (11:20-25)   41
Jesus' Authority is Questioned (11:27-33)   42

Chapter Twelve

The Parable of the Wicked Tenants (12:1-12)   42
The Question about Paying Taxes (12:13-17)   43
The Question about the Resurrection (12:18-27)   43
The First Commandment (12:28-34)   44
The Question about David's Son (12:35-37)   45
Jesus Denounces the Scribes (12:38-40)   45
The Widow's Offering (12:41-44)   45

Chapter Thirteen

The Destruction of the Temple Foretold (13:1-8)   46
Persecution Foretold (13:9-13)   46
The Desolating Sacrilege (13:14-23)   47
The Coming of the Son of Man (13:24-27)   47
The Lesson of the Fig Tree (13:28-31)   48
The Necessity for Watchfulness (13:32-37)   48

Chapter Fourteen

The Plot to Kill Jesus (14:1-2)   49
The Anointing at Bethany (14:3-9)   49
Judas Agrees to Betray Jesus (14:10-11)   49
The Passover with the Disciples (14:12-21)   50
The Institution of the Lord's Supper (14:22-25)   50
Peter's Denial Foretold (14:26-31)   50
Jesus Prays in Gethsemane (14:32-42)   51
The Betrayal and Arrest of Jesus (14:43-52)   52
Jesus before the Council (14:53-65)   52
Peter Denies Jesus (14:66-72)   53

Chapter Fifteen

Jesus before Pilate (15:1-5)   54
Pilate Hands Jesus over to Be Crucified (15:6-15)   54
The Soldiers Mock Jesus (15:16-20)   55
The Crucifixion of Jesus (15:21-32)   56
The Death of Jesus (15:33-41)   58
The Burial of Jesus (15:42-47)   58

Chapter Sixteen

The Resurrection of Jesus (16:1-8)   60
Jesus Appears to Mary Magdalene (16:9-11)   60
Jesus Appears to Two Disciples (16:12-13)   61
Jesus Commissions the Disciples (16:14-18)   61
The Ascension of Jesus (16:19-20)   61